REGGAE
Sierra Wilson
MY FAVORITE MUSIC
AV2
www.openlightbox.com

AV2

Step 1
Go to **www.openlightbox.com**

Step 2
Enter this unique code
WQGLRDNE2

Step 3
Explore your interactive eBook!

AV2 is optimized for use on any device

Your interactive eBook comes with...

- **Read — Audio**: Listen to the entire book read aloud
- **Videos**: Watch informative video clips
- **Weblinks**: Gain additional information for research
- **Try This!**: Complete activities and hands-on experiments
- **Key Words**: Study vocabulary, and complete a matching word activity
- **Quizzes**: Test your knowledge
- **Slideshows**: View images and captions
- **Share**: Share titles within your Learning Management System (LMS) or Library Circulation System
- **Citation**: Create bibliographical references following APA, CMOS, and MLA styles

This title is part of our AV2 digital subscription

1-Year K–5 Subscription
ISBN 978-1-7911-3320-7

Access hundreds of AV2 titles with our digital subscription.
Sign up for a FREE trial at **www.openlightbox.com/trial**

The digital components of this book are guaranteed to stay active for at least five years from the date of publication.

REGGAE

Contents

I love music.

Reggae is my favorite kind of music.

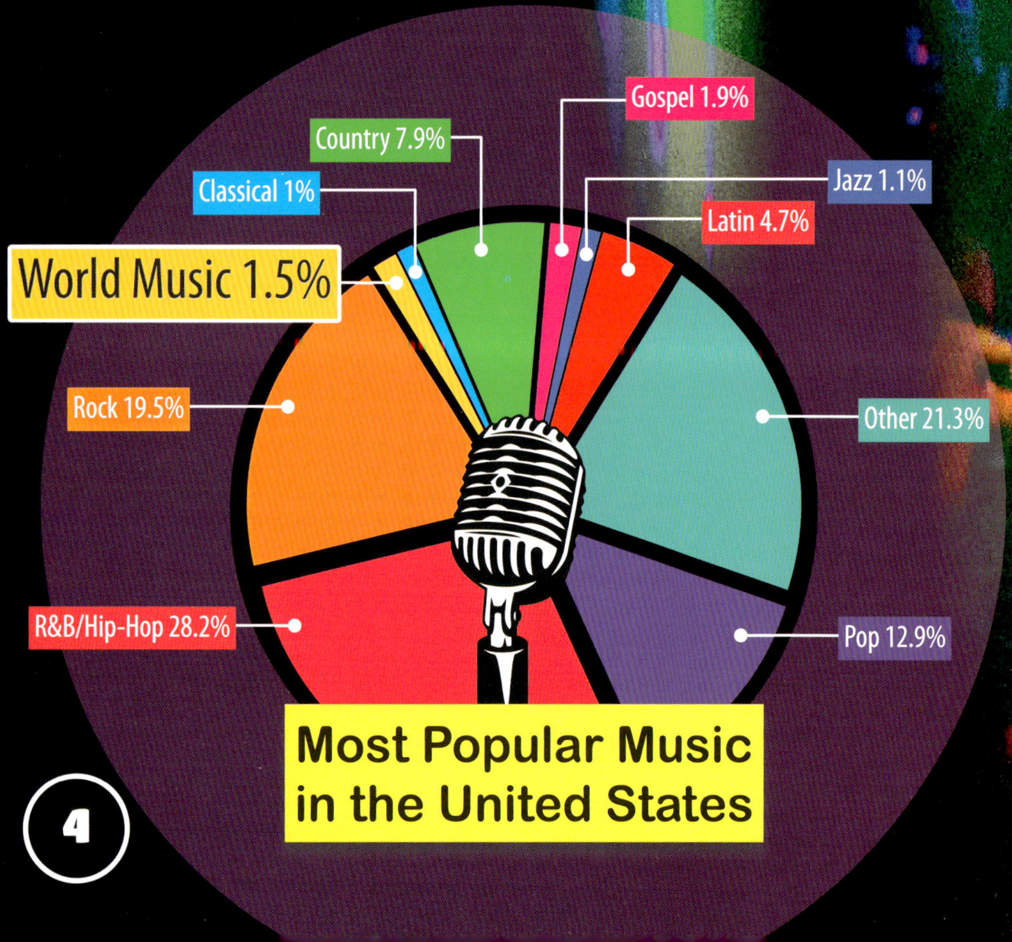

Reggae music was first made in Jamaica in the 1960s.

Reggae comes from other kinds of Jamaican music.

It also mixes in music from Africa and the United States.

The first reggae artists all came from Jamaica.

Bob Marley helped reggae become popular around the world.

Reggae singers use a style called singjay.

This means they only sing some words.

Other words are spoken over the beat of the song.

Most reggae songs talk about problems in the world.

They encourage people to help each other.

Drums and bass guitars play an important role in reggae music.

These two instruments give reggae its strong beat.

I like to play reggae music with my friends.

Each person has a role to play.

Playing in a band teaches us how to work together.

Reggae can now be heard around the world.

The world's largest reggae festival is held in Benicàssim, Spain.

Close to 250,000 people go to this festival every year.

I love reggae music.

It makes me want to move and groove.

REGGAE FACTS

These pages provide detailed information that expands on the interesting facts found in the book. They are intended to be used by adults as a learning support to help young readers round out their knowledge of each musical genre featured in the *My Favorite Music* series.

Pages 4–5

I love music. Reggae is my favorite kind of music. Music is the name given to sounds made with voices or musical instruments and put together in a way that conveys emotion. People use music to express themselves. Music is a form of cultural heritage. Different forms of music are connected to the history and culture of the people who created these forms. Listening to reggae music is one way to learn about Jamaica's culture and history.

Pages 6–7

Reggae comes from other kinds of Jamaican music. Jamaica gained independence from Great Britain in 1962. The years following independence were marked by both hope and struggles. Reggae music partly reflects the efforts of Jamaicans to separate from British culture and celebrate their African heritage. It evolved mostly from the Caribbean music styles known as ska and rocksteady. Over time, American styles of music, such as R&B and jazz, began to be integrated into some reggae music.

Pages 8–9

The first reggae artists all came from Jamaica. Members of the Rastafari religion were some of the first reggae musicians. Rastafari started in Jamaica in the 1930s. Its beliefs mix mysticism, pan-Africanism, and Christianity. From the Rastafari viewpoint, Black people around the world are exiles, waiting for deliverance. Many themes from Rastafari beliefs are reflected in reggae songs. Bob Marley began his music career as a ska musician. He went on to play reggae music with rock elements that appealed to a wide audience.

Pages 10–11

Reggae singers use a style called singjay. The word is a combination of "singing" and "deejaying." Singjay involves not only singing but toasting, or lyrically chanting, the words. When chanting, a vocalist talks over the beat of the music in a manner similar to rapping. Reggae is also mostly sung with a Jamaican accent, noting the origins of the music.

Pages 12–13

Most reggae songs talk about problems in the world. After Jamaica gained independence, political parties fought for power. Urban areas suffered from violence and economic problems. Many reggae songs reflect the struggles of this time period. A variety of global social issues, ranging from racism to oppression, have also been addressed in the music. Still, the driving theme behind reggae music is one of love and unity. The songs encourage people to stand and work together when facing a threat or problem.

Pages 14–15

Drums and bass guitars play an important role in reggae music. Musical groups often use a variety of instruments to produce layered, complex sounds. To produce its strong rhythm, reggae music uses the bass guitar, along with a variety of different percussion instruments. The bass guitar is key to reggae as it provides the music with its signature groove. It is often considered reggae's lead instrument as a result.

Pages 16–17

I like to play reggae music with my friends. Creating music with others helps teach children cooperation, teamwork, and how to achieve goals. Children who regularly play music tend to have more confidence and get along better with others. Some students learn better in groups because they do not feel the pressure of having to learn on their own.

Pages 18–19

Reggae can now be heard around the world. It is popular not only in Jamaica, but in many other countries as well. In fact, the world's largest reggae festival is held not in Jamaica, but in Spain. The week-long Rototom Sunsplash takes place every August in Benicàssim, Spain. Close to 250,000 people attend in person, with another 3 million viewers tuning in online.

Pages 20–21

I love reggae music. Recent studies suggest that learning and practicing music can be beneficial to a child's ability to learn. Among these benefits are improved motor skills and dexterity, increased test scores, and even raised Intelligence Quotient, or IQ, scores. Learning music at an early age has also been shown to aid in language development and to improve reading and listening skills.

SIGHT WORDS

Research has shown that as much as 65 percent of all written material published in English is made up of 300 words. These 300 words cannot be taught using pictures or learned by sounding them out. They must be recognized by sight. This book contains 66 common sight words to help young readers improve their reading fluency and comprehension. This book also teaches young readers several important content words. These words are paired with pictures to aid in learning and improve understanding.

Page	Sight Words First Appearance
4	country, I, in, is, kind, most, my, of, other, states, the, world
5	first, made, was
6	comes, from
7	also, and, it
8	all, came
9	around
10	a, use
11	are, means, only, over, some, song, they, this, words
12	about, talk
13	each, help, one, people, to
14	an, important, play
15	give, its, these, two
16	each, has, like, with
17	how, together, us, work
18	be, can
19	close, every, go, year
21	makes, me, move, want

Page	Content Words First Appearance
4	classical, gospel, hip-hop, jazz, Latin, music, pop, R&B, reggae, rock, United States
5	Jamaica
7	Africa
8	artists
9	Bob Marley
10	singers, singjay, style
11	beat
12	problems
14	bass guitars, drums, role
15	instruments
16	friends, person
17	band
18	Benicàssim, festival, Spain

Published by Lightbox Learning Inc.
276 5th Avenue, Suite 704 #917
New York, NY 10001
Website: www.openlightbox.com

Library of Congress Cataloging-in-Publication Data
Names: Wilson, Sierra, author.
Title: Reggae / Sierra Wilson.
Description: New York : Lightbox Learning Inc., 2026. | Series: My favorite music | Audience: Grades 2-3
Identifiers: LCCN 2024048621 (print) | LCCN 2024048622 (ebook) | ISBN 9798874503789 (library binding) | ISBN 9798874503796 (paperback) | ISBN 9798874503802 (ebook other) | ISBN 9798874503826 (ebook other)
Subjects: LCSH: Reggae (Music)--History and criticism--Juvenile literature.
Classification: LCC ML3532 .W58 2025 (print) | LCC ML3532 (ebook) | DDC 782.421646--dc23/eng 20241015
LC record available at https://lccn.loc.gov/2024048621
LC ebook record available at https://lccn.loc.gov/2024048622

Printed in Guangzhou, China
1 2 3 4 5 6 7 8 9 0 29 28 27 26 25

042025
100924

Art Director: Terry Paulhus **Project Coordinator:** Heather Kissock